P9-DHQ-180

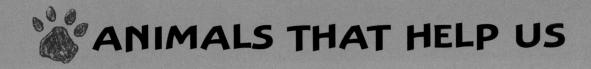

Animals on the Farm

Sally Morgan

FRANKLIN WATTS
A Division of Grolier Publishing
NEW YORK • LONDON • HONG KONG • SYDNEY
DANBURY, CONNECTICUT

Picture Credits:

Cover: Holt Studios International (Wayne Hutchison)

Interior Pictures: Bruce Coleman p. 27b; Ecoscene p. 16
(James Marchington), 26b (Paul Ferraby); Eye
Ubiquitous p. 7b (L. Fordyce); Werner Forman Archive
p. 4 (British Museum, London); Robert Harding pp. 9t
(Liba Taylor), 11b (Adam Woolfitt), 22, 23b (Christopher
Rennie), 27t; Holt Studios International pp. 5b (Sarah
Rowland), 6t (Bob Gibbons), 12 (Sarah Rowland), 13t
(Dick Roberts), 14t (Phil McLean), 17t (John Adams), 21t
(Nigel Cattlin), 23t (Nigel Cattlin), 24t (Jean Hall), 26t
(Nigel Cattlin); Hutchison Library pp. 9b (Jeremy
Horner), 20b (Tony Souter); Frank Lane Picture Agency
pp. 15t (A. Parker), 18t (Roger Tidman), 18b (David
Dalton), 19b (Roger Tidman), 20t (Life Science Images),
24b (Jm Fichaux/Sunset), 25b (M.J. Thomas), 28 (Peter
Dean), 29t (M.J. Thomas); Natural History
Photographic Agency pp. 10 (R. Sorensen & J. Olsen),
14b (E. A. Janes), 15b (Yves Lanceau); Oxford Scientific
Films p. 17b (Lon. E. Lauber), 21b (Clive Bromhall);
Panos Pictures p. 29b (J-L Dugast); Rex Features p. 13b
(Vic Thomason); Rural History Centre, University of
Reading p. 8 (Eric Guy Collection/DX289/1001); Still
Pictures pp. 5t (Nigel Dickinson), 6b (Mark Edwards), 7t
(Jorgen Schytte), 11t (Thomas Raupach), 19t
(Klein/Hubert), 25t (Hartmut Schwarzbach).

Series editor: Helen Lanz
Series designer: Louise Snowdon
Picture research: Sue Mennell

First published in 1999 by Franklin Watts

First American edition 1999 by Franklin Watts
A Division of Grolier Publishing
90 Sherman Turnpike
Danbury, CT 06816

Visit Franklin Watts/Children's Press on the Internet at:
http://publishing.grolier.com

A catalog record for this title is available from the
Library of Congress.

ISBN: 0-531-14565-4 (lib. bdg)   0-531-15407-6 (pbk)

Contents

Working Animals

For thousands of years, people have used animals to help them with their farming. Horses, oxen, yaks, and dogs are among the animals that have been domesticated, or tamed, to share the work in the fields.

This ancient Egyptian painting shows a cat helping its master hunt and catch birds.

One of the very first animals that helped the farmer was the cat. As long ago as 2000 B.C., the ancient Egyptians used cats to catch mice in their granaries, the buildings where they stored their grain.

In some countries, tractors and other machines have replaced animals. But despite these changes, animals still have an important role in farming.

This combine harvester cuts and thrashes grain, reducing the work of the farmer.

Horses and oxen are still used to help with farmwork today. They pull carts and plows and move heavy loads. Dogs are useful, too, helping round up other animals, such as sheep.

Animals are also kept for food — eggs, milk, and meat. Other animals are kept because their skins and wool are used to make clothing.

Animals as Machines

In many countries, horses, mules, and dogs are still used on farms. In Asia, farm animals include oxen and water buffalo, while in the mountains of South America, people rely on yaks and llamas.

Most of these animals are chosen because they are strong and they have stamina — they can work long hours without getting tired.

These oxen in India are being used to lift water from a well to pipe to nearby fields.

In some countries, farmers cannot afford expensive farm machinery. They rely on animals to do the heavy work. Sometimes animals are better than machines. In the mountains where the tracks are too steep for tractors, only animals can move across the land.

These terraces are too steep and narrow for a tractor.

Animal Anecdote

In some parts of the world, people have chosen not to use modern machines. The Amish people of North America are traditional farmers. They still use horses for plowing on their farms, and they take their crops to market in horse-drawn carts.

Working the Fields

A lot of work has to be done before a farmer can harvest his crops. Each year, the soil has to be plowed — this breaks up the earth. Then it is harrowed to make the soil even so that the seeds can be planted successfully.

Plowing and harrowing are hard work. They are jobs that can be done by big, powerful tractors, but in many countries, animals, including horses, oxen, and buffalo, still pull the tools used to do this.

Traditionally, horses were used to pull plows and harrows — the tools used to turn or break up the soil.

This farmer in India is using oxen to help him harrow his land.

Rice is grown in flooded fields called paddies. The ground is wet, so it is impossible for a tractor to drive on the land. Instead, farmers use water buffalo. Although the buffalo is a heavy animal, it has wide feet that help it move across the waterlogged soil.

Paddy fields are so full of water that a tractor would sink in the soft mud.

The Roundup

Often farmers have to move groups of animals from one place to another — and it is not easy. With the help of a well-trained dog or a surefooted horse, a farmer or cowboy can control his or her livestock more easily.

Many dogs have been bred to herd or drive animals such as sheep, cattle, and horses. Cattle dogs are used to control herds that roam freely on unfenced land. These dogs drive the cattle by biting at their heels, so they are called heelers. Dogs that move the herd forward are known as drivers.

Sheepdogs are herding dogs that are used to round up sheep and move them from one place to another.

Some dogs are used to protect the sheep. They stay with the flock night and day, guarding them from foxes and wolves.

This German farmer and his dogs watch over their flock.

Horses are used on the huge cattle ranches of Argentina and the United States. The cowboys and horses work closely together to round up the herds of beef cattle.

The horses are used to being close to cattle. They have to be surefooted and nimble so they can twist this way and that as they chase the herd.

The cowboys could use jeeps, but they would not be able to get as close to the cattle or change direction as quickly.

Dog Control

Many sheep are kept on large mountain farms where they are free to roam the hillsides. A farmer needs the help of a sheepdog to move the flocks.

One of the best-known sheepdog breeds is the Border Collie.

A puppy starts its training when the farmer takes it into a field with a few sheep. The puppy is placed on one side of the sheep and the farmer stands on the opposite side. Then the puppy is called.

As the dog goes toward the farmer, the sheep move forward, too. The puppy learns quickly that it can make the sheep move by walking toward them.

Sheepdogs often control sheep by staring at them. They also watch the sheep closely and move quickly to stop a sheep from going in the wrong direction. Often the farmer is a long way from the dog, so the dog is controlled by hand signals and whistles.

Animal Anecdote

Sheepdogs have natural herding skills. Border Collies especially love to herd things. If there are no sheep around, they will try to herd people, other dogs, cats, birds, and even vacuum cleaners and lawn mowers. In fact, they will try to herd anything that moves!

The Rat-Catchers

Rats and mice cause farmers lots of problems. They chew through wood and wire and damage stores of grain. They can also carry diseases. Both rats and mice give birth to young every few weeks, so they have to be controlled.

Cats have excellent eyesight. This makes them good hunters of rats and mice, so they are popular animals on farms.

Rats and mice are considered pests by farmers.

Terrier dogs are small but strong, and they love hunting. They are also natural rat-catchers. They have powerful jaws and can kill a rat by biting through its neck.

Because of their small size, Terriers can squeeze into small holes to chase out rats.

Wild animals can also help the farmer. Owls feed on rats and mice, so some farmers encourage these birds to nest in their barns.

Owls hunt at night. Their excellent sense of hearing allows them to catch mice and rats as they move about the farm in the dark.

Animal Anecdote

Towser the farm cat is a record-breaker. She was an expert mouse-catcher who lived to the great age of 24. During her life, she caught nearly 29,000 mice. That works out to three mice a day!

Hunt, Point, Retrieve

Hunting is part of farming life. Farmers who choose to hunt often use dogs to help them. The dogs drive out the game (the animal being hunted) and collect it once it has been shot.

The breed of dog used depends on the type of animal being hunted and the job the dog is needed for. Some gundogs, such as Weimaraners, can hunt, or search, for the game, point to where the game is, and then retrieve, or fetch, it.

Other dogs, such as Golden Retrievers and Labradors, are used mainly to fetch the game once it is on the ground.

Gundogs have to sniff out the game once it has been shot down.

Animal Anecdote

The Chesapeake Bay Retriever is a well-known gundog from Maryland. These dogs have a thick, oily coat that keeps them warm when they jump into freezing cold water to retrieve game, such as duck.

Trained to the Gun

Gundogs have an excellent sense of smell. This means they can follow the scent of game through fields and woodlands.

When a gundog finds the scent of a bird, it follows the trail until it finds the bird itself. Then the dog stands still, marking the position of the game.

Some dogs follow scent on the ground, while others track smells in the air. Then they point at the game.

Some skills are natural, but gundogs, like sheepdogs, have to be trained. Puppies start their training when they are a few months old. They are given basic obedience training, when they learn to sit, come, and stay. The puppies are also taught to run off in a certain direction to find or fetch the game.

The dogs are then taught to retrieve a sausage-shaped object called a dummy. As they become more skilled, they have to fetch dummies hidden in grass or that have been thrown into water.

Later, the dogs are taught to pick up a bird that has been shot and carry it back to their owners without damaging it. They are taught to drop the bird, too!

Animals for Food

Animals don't just help farmers move heavy loads or round up other animals. They are also important because they provide us with food. These foods include meat, eggs, fish, milk, and cheese.

Chickens are common farm animals and are seen in farmyards all over the world. They provide us with eggs and meat. They are easy to look after and can be kept in pens on even the smallest farms.

Cows, goats, and sheep provide us with milk. After giving birth to their young, the mothers produce milk for several months. Farmers take the milk once the calf has been weaned. It can be drunk or made into cheese or yogurt.

It's not just large animals that provide us with food. Bees collect pollen from flowers and turn it into honey. We have learned how to collect this so we can eat it.

Animal Anecdote

Some animals can be used to help us find food. Pigs are used in France to sniff out a type of mushroom called a truffle. Truffles are a special food and are worth a lot of money. In the fall, keepers take their pigs into woodland. The pigs' snouts are so sensitive they can find the truffles under the ground.

21

Something to Wear

Woolen clothes, such as sweaters and socks, help keep us warm. We also use leather to make clothes, as well as shoes and bags.

In this factory, clean, washed wool is put onto spindles. The wool is then ready to be used to make clothes.

Wool comes from a number of different animals, including sheep and goats. The animals' thick fleeces keep them warm during the winter months. In the summer, they molt, or lose their wool, so they don't overheat. Thousands of years ago, people learned that they could cut off this wool and use it to make clothes.

It's not just sheep and goats that provide us with wool. Alpacas, vicunas, llamas, and rabbits have long hair that can be made into woolen clothes, too. Fine wool such as cashmere comes from goats living in India. It is used to make shawls and sweaters. Mohair, another expensive wool, comes from the angora goat and rabbit.

The wool from this angora goat is used to make high-quality clothes.

Leather comes from the skins of animals such as cattle and oxen. It's a tough material that does not wear out quickly.

The animal skin has to go through many different stages before the leather can be used.

Sheepshearing

Sheep are sheared in order to give us wool to make clothes. Shearing starts in early summer before it gets too hot. In some countries sheepshearers cut the wool using hand shears. In richer countries, the shearers often use electric shears, which cut the wool close to the skin.

As much as 40lb (18kg) of wool can be shorn from the largest sheep.

The shearers try to get the fleece off in one piece. Before it can be made into clothes, it has to be washed and untangled. It can be dyed to produce different-colored wools. It is then spun into long lengths.

Some breeds of sheep produce long hair, which makes high-quality woolen cloth. One of the finest wools comes from the merino sheep. Its wool is extremely soft. The merino sheep originally came from Spain, but now it is found all around the world. Mountain sheep produce coarse, short hairs. This wool is used to make carpets and cheaper woolen suits and socks.

The wool is graded. The longest hairs may be 20in (50cm) in length — these make the best wool.

Animal Anecdote

There are many millions of sheep in Australia, so sheepshearing is a big operation. Teams of sheepshearers travel from farm to farm, shearing the flocks. Some of the top sheepshearers can shear as many as 800 sheep in a day.

Farmyard Smells!

Many people turn their noses up at the smell of manure. But this smelly waste is very useful. It is full of nutrients. These nutrients are used by plants to help them grow. Farmers spread animal manure over their fields to fertilize them in order to make their crops grow as large as possible.

Animal manure helps put goodness back in the soil.

Farmyard manure from stables is a mix of straw and droppings. It can't go straight onto the fields. Instead, it has to be allowed to age. As the manure ages, it rots and can be spread onto the fields in spring.

A pile of fresh manure is hot and produces lots of steam.

In some countries, animal droppings are used as a fuel. In India, there is a shortage of wood to burn on fires and in ovens. Instead, people collect animal droppings, which they dry in the sun. The dried dung can then be put on fires as if it were wood.

Animal Anecdote

Some animal dung has a very powerful smell. People have tried using lion dung to keep deer and rabbits out of their gardens and crops. These animals smell the dung and are tricked into thinking that there is a large and dangerous lion about, so they stay away!

Farming in the Future

Farming has changed a lot, especially over the last 100 years. Many powerful machines have replaced the work of animals on the farm. But these machines are expensive and not always suited to all types of farmland.

A tractor can do the work of many horses in a much shorter time.

Recently, people have become concerned about how food is produced and how the land is treated.

Animals have been bred to give us more eggs or more milk, or to be bigger so they provide us with more meat. Chemicals have been sprayed onto crops to give bigger harvests.

Some farmers are returning to traditional methods of farming.

Modern farming will always use new, powerful machines, but animals still help us on farms all over the world. We need them for many foods and for many materials to make our clothes. And farmers still need their help with heavy farmwork and to look after other farm animals.

Glossary

chemical   an artificial liquid or powder made in a factory to spray or sprinkle on crops to kill pests or make the crop grow bigger

combine harvester   a machine that cuts crops, separating the grain from the stalks

fleece   a sheep's coat of wool

livestock   farm animals

nutrients   the goodness in the manure that gives plants and crops the necessary food to grow

obedience   willing to do what one is told

pest   an animal that damages crops

pollen   the yellow dust that can be found on a flower

terrace   a small flat piece of land on a hillside, like a step

traditional   an old way of doing something

wean   when a baby or young animal moves from drinking milk to eating solid food

Useful addresses

Animal Place
3448 Laguna Creek Trail
Vacaville, CS 95688-9724
http://www.animalplace.org/

A permanent refuge for abused and disgarded farm animals.

Animal Welfare Institute
P.O. Box 3650
Washington, DC 20007
http://www.animalwelfare.com/

Works for the ending of cruel treatment of farm animals.

Farm Sanctuary
P.O. Box 150
Watkins Glen, NY 14891
http://www.farmsanctuary.org/

Operates farm animal sanctuaries and works to stop abuse of animals raised for food.

PETA
People for the Ethical Treatment of Animals
501 Front Street
Norfolk, VA 23510
http://www.peta—online.org/

Largest animal rights organization in the world.

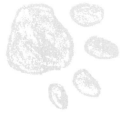

Index